A DREAM
A PRAYER
AND COWBOY

TRACY HAMMOND- TELLING IT LIKE IT IS

ACKNOWLEDGEMENT

It is with heartfelt Gratitude that I thank God for blessing me with all of these experiences, these people, and these specific animals in my life. For the Dreams he's placed in my heart and the guts to chase em'.

My best friend and husband, Jason, for all of his support and patience with all of us horse crazy girls.

For Gini Roberge for pushing me to complete this book, helping me every step of the way, and capturing these amazing shots of Cowboy and his Cowgirls. I Love her authentic passion for horses and the families that revolve their lives around them. For Gini's artistic ability to capture the moment like very few can. It, in itself is poetic.

ISBN-13: 978-1541006164

ISBN-10: 154100616X

To my Mom and Dad who brought me up loving animals and "Telling it like it is".

CONTENTS

BUCKAROO MY ASS   Pg #1

THANK GOD FOR ARENA DIRT   Pg #9

I SAW GOD TODAY   Pg #12

MY FIRST BARREL RACE   Pg #16

COWBOY   Pg #20

KIONA'S DESTINY   Pg #25

JUST LET HER RIDE   Pg #33

COUNTRY LIVIN'   Pg #36

AND GOD MADE A HORSE   Pg #38

IN THIS ARENA DIRT   Pg #43

IT WAS QUITE A SPOT…   Pg #46

ABOUT THE AUTHOR   Pg #48

CHAPTER ONE- BUCKAROO MY ASS

(The air was cool and crisp this morning like a fall day, Beau, Zip, and I were blessed to go ride out in the wide open of the wheat fields and it reminded me of this experience of a life time I thought I'd share with you. An Experience that I'm feared my 3 year old daughter may never get a chance to see.)

It was fall, I was twenty years old, and I'd just moved to Golconda, Nevada with my soon to be husband to live on the family Ranch. It was time to head up on the "mountain" and gather and push cows down on the flat. I will try to illustrate as best as I can a vision that is like none that I've ever seen before. Jason and I lived at Red House Ranch which is the first of the 3 Ranches that Hammond Ranches owned. It took 45 minutes to drive from "Red House Ranch" to the main Ranch, "Jake's Creek", that is how much land they owned and then their BLM land stretched all the way to the Idaho border along the Owyhee Desert. Let me remind you that in Northern Nevada it literally takes about 30 acres to feed one cow and they ran approximately 2500 head. Ok - bear with me now, I want to give you an idea of the lay of the land, this is where the story gets good and when I think of it, it brings tears to my eyes.

They said we'd be up at Buckaroo Camp about a week. As Jason, his uncle Lynn, and I, loaded our mounts from Red House Ranch and drove down the flat to Jake's Creek. Johnny Horton was cranked on that little cassette player in Lynn's old Ford Pickup it was early in the morning and the sun had still not risen. I could not possibly have any idea what was in store for my week ahead.

We arrived at Jake's Creek, unloaded our "cavi" (some call a remuda but in Nevada it's a cavi). We saddled our horses. I made sure I saddled my good rope horse. Apparently the ritual was to turn your "Cavi" out from the corral at Jake's Creek and those horses would run all the way to Buckaroo Camp. Now, I knew good and well that there were wild mustangs out there in that country and there was no way I was taking a chance on my expensive rope horse deciding he'd like to run "wild & free." In all I believe we had about 20 head in our string. You needed to take at least 3 horses per person we'd be riding long days and they would need a day of rest. So that is exactly what we did. Uncle Lynn was riding this mare they had picked up off of the track, he was packing a stock whip and I was thinking hmm, ok, I'll just sit back and watch the show? Our cinches were tight, hats down tight, and rooty, toot, they opened that corral gate. Those horses took off down that trail to Buckaroo Camp on a dead run like they knew exactly where they were headed. "Mack" was in the lead it certainly wasn't his first trip to Camp. We followed them for probably a mile or half mile up this steep, rocky, mountain. I felt like I'd just stepped in a time machine and somehow wound up on the set of a John Wayne filming, we were only lacking kayaying Indians and gun shots. It was western. After a while we backed our horses down to a long trot and Uncle Lynn said we wouldn't see them again until we arrived at camp. Yes, I was thinking those horses have no one following or guiding them and they'll show up right at camp? But, the Mustangs? What about the mustangs? Will they try to put them in their band?

We are riding along this trail with wide open sky, big, green, lush pastures, and huge mountain peaks with snow still on top of them. Uncle Lynn showing us the "brood mare" pasture. A place where their great uncle Phil used to train mounts for the Calvary. I'm talking this is country that no one has been in but, buckaroos, Indians, mustangs and wild cattle. You could feel it in the air and so could the animals. Just riding along the trail you'd find arrow heads. I'm not making this up, those arrow heads were sitting there just the way some Indian had dropped it years ago.

We finally arrived at camp and yes the "cavi" was there. They were standing at the Barb wire gate to this large round corral built with willow twigs, hog wire, barb wire, mesh, whatever any buckaroo from the last 30 years could find to build it with. Honestly I thought there is no way I'm putting my "good horse" in that corral and I was searching for a good tree and he might just be tied up for the week! I did end up putting him in the corral with the rest of the herd and he made it all week without a scratch.

There was a tin cabin there and that would be the base. I guess the famous Claude Dallas hid out there at one point and time. When you walked in you could certainly feel a presence there of all who'd come before. The Whiskey was brought out and as we sat at the camp table the tales were started. Two in particular about some rabid coyotes and the ghost of a lost Indian maiden that sings in the wind. I know from then on when I went out in the dark to hide behind a sage brush our little, mean, border collie, Willie was called to my side. It's an uneasy feeling when your pants are down, it's dark, you can hear the coyotes; and your darn black and white companion tucks tail and heads back for the cabin!

Morning couldn't come soon enough it was freezing cold in that little canvas teepee tent. Jason and I huddled in that bedroll with the dog, Willie. We, all three were shivering as we got up and put our boots on. I walked outside to see we had acquired about 1/2 " of snow thru the night. I was grateful that tarp had been thrown over our saddles. Morning chores were done and it was time to catch and saddle our mounts and take care of the job at hand. I could hear a ruckus coming from the corral area and Jason's voice raised, as I came around the corner I could see all the horses in a dead run going round and round that tiny corral and Jason's trusty mount, Rio was running around with them only outside the corral. Apparently he saw Jason with a halter in his hand and jumped the corral. As the week drew on I learned that was just a daily thing and I'd get used to it.

We were finally saddled and on a long trot to find the first group of cows out on the desert. Uncle Lynn advised that no matter how gentle a horse was if you had them at buckaroo camp to hang on because they all seemed to have a buck in them. I perked my ears because so far he'd been right on the money. By mid-morning the terrain had changed drastically and I could actually see the BLM/Idaho border fence line, we were out there in God's country and there are no words, nor camera that could capture the feeling, the air, and the portrait that is forever painted in my memory. I was riding this long legged, dun horse named Sunny. He was fast, and cowy, and I had a snaffle bit on him. He didn't have much of a mouth so stopping did not come quickly but, hey we had the whole country side to stop? Most of the cattle out there had never seen a human but, they were used to horses because they shared the desert with the mustang and antelope. In Nevada when gathering it's a good idea to pack a good pair of binoculars with you, from afar sometimes you can't tell if it's a cow or a mustang. Just to get you a feel for it, it was cool and brisk, the wind was blowing at least 30 miles an hour, the horses were blowing and snorting, if a cow saw you they were on a dead run. I'm talking long horned 2 year old oreanas.

(oreana is one that is unbranded) Sunny, this horse I was on like to jumped sage brush too, so it was western but, not Strawberry Roan western thank goodness. Jason and I came down this little hill and out there in the 30 mile an hour wind was something I'd never felt or seen in my life. On one side were 40 head of mustang mares and colts their manes and tales blowing in the wind as they all stood and looked at us with their ears perked. Down below them were about 20 head of wild cows. Another 30 foot beside them was a herd of 200 antelope. If I hadn't seen it with my own eyes I'd never believe it was true. We both just kind of sat there in awe, looked at one another like well? Let's do it, and we headed for that little band of wild cows. We went right thru that herd of antelope so close to them I could've roped one and I was packing, and don't think it didn't cross my mind either! So Jason and I finally get around this group of cows to start pushing them towards the mountain. Of course they scattered every direction. Jason and Willie headed left, old jumping sage brush, Sunny, and I headed right and I mean on a dead run, no mouth, snaffle bit, right after those wild steers, jumping sage brush all the way. Casey Tibbs eat your heart out. I really thought after the first few sage brush jumps it'd stop but, it never really did and I just decided to enjoy the ride. I think my legs were a little raw and sore by the time we made it back to the ole tin cabin though.

  What a fun week it was. Cold but, always exciting one day we had a 2 year old mustang, stud colt follow us all way back to camp, another day we had a weanling colt that could barely walk on 3 legs, poor, and sad. I learned a lot about the "mystic, wild, mustang," the media portrays on TV. The last day we gathered in a snow blizzard Jason sang Chris Ledoux Songs all the way back to camp on a long trot, I just put my head down so my hat would block the freezing wind, dropped my reins and let James take me back to camp.

On the way home we turned those horses out just like we did in the beginning only this time we didn't even try to follow them for a while. Uncle Lynn said they'd be waiting for us at the gate at Jake's Creek. Again it was just the 3 of us Lynn, Jason, & I riding back to the home ranch. Once again I was on my rope horse, James (I still wasn't taking a chance of him gathering up with those mustangs or worse picking a fight with a renegade 2 year old stud colt). Of course we had to make some stops Jason and Lynn or both had a stash of some sort of brandy with them to keep them "warm". We had hit a spot in the trail the ground was ok, so I said "let's race" and I took off. They soon joined & they were eating my dust pretty good. The trail became rocky and of course I slowed ole James right down, Lynn and Jason barreled right on by me. I was thinking geesh kind of hard on horse flesh aren't ya? Apparently you don't race a "Ranch" horse because they don't really have a stop? How was I to know?

What an experience. I'm sorry to say they sold out the Ranch in 98 and it will forever be a special spot in my heart and soul. Have a great day!

Love,
Tracy D. (written by Tracy Hammond August 29, 2011) ode to the Quarter Circle TJ □

7

CHAPTER TWO- THANK GOD FOR ARENA DIRT

I was doing laundry today and I thought these socks are so stained there is no way I can get out this 'Arena Dirt" and then I thought….

'Thank God for Arena Dirt'

By Tracy D. Hammond

A place where there is no time for texting, emails, Facebook, and the WII - not even reality TV.

Just hard work, sweat, try & grit …. Practicing to be the best you can be.

The laughter and fun, so many friends made, some marriages and funerals held on this earthly floor,

The goose bumps, tears, cheers, blood, and some visions that'll give ya chills to the core.

"Yep," good ole fashioned arena dirt.

A place to spend quality time with your children and family.

I thought about how many stories could be told from arena dirt?

The adrenalin of roping fast calves, making quick turns, 100 point rides, and of course the buck offs that leave ya in a world of hurt.

You know I've seen it all from "perfect ground" (if there is such a thing to a barrel racer) to deep sand, and the MUD! It's all still that Arena Dirt.

That stuff that keeps our horses sound and fuels our passions.

Keeps us all taking the risks and challenges instead of sitting on the couch and staying up with the latest fashions.

So many life lessons have been taught right here in this arena dust.

Never quit, some days you may win, some you may lose but, if you work hard enough and believe you will succeed. And with your fate, in GOD you must trust.

So yes, I Thank God for this this arena dirt,

Even if it stains my good socks and favorite white T-shirt.

CHAPTER THREE- I SAW GOD TODAY

Amen~ I was walking down to feed tonight with this beautiful sky; painted better than any portrait or photograph. As I walked I thought of the questions asked of me in the last 5 years. Is the sacrifice worth it? The vet bills, hay, and all the extra bills that go along with property and animals. I've been asked "what I do all day anyway?" We've been called "sadistic" for naming the steers we intended to butcher "Six, "Red", and "Brindle" ("Six" had the ear tag "#736" he was black and out of cow #736 who's calves' have won many a Asotin County Fair, and of course "Red" because he was Red, Brindle because he was "Brindle".)I walked down to feed the 2.5 head of horses, 9 hens, and however many wild barn cats we have. I thought about how our vet bills are a minimum because we strive to take care of our animals and do preventative maintenance.

I paused and thought of Utah, the 10 year old gelding we raised and had to bury this spring. It was all too clear in my memory that night, pouring down rain and cold. Calling Dr. Rustebakke for the 2nd time that night to come and put him down because he was in so much pain. I can still hear that diesel revving as it came down that gravel road. Dave, showing up like "dad" to help. Not just the local vet but, family, who shows up when you need them the most.

The many cold mornings and nights in the last 5 years I've bundled TJ up and put her in the stroller to go feed, and put out the chimney fire. Taking the weed burner to the frozen faucet to water the horses and the constant mud, dust, and dirt that plagues this home. The drool that the little dog, Willie Jack, leaves on the living room windows, the dog hair.... so much dog hair. The mud room cat and mascot Belle, who sometimes pees on my favorite practice rope and on top of the washing machine! UGH. Packing wood, packing 50 pound sacks of grain across the pasture to feed the pigs. I put a dent in our fancy pickup to unload the $45.00 pigs.

Then I just smiled and thought, yes. Yes, thank God we live the way we do. I thought of the life lessons TJ has learned already at age 5. Cleaning the chicken coop, planting vegetables, (which I'm still learning). She knows her flowers she will "shut the gate behind her." The love these animals all have to give. The fact that TJ can run the Excavator and showed me how to dig the hole to bury the goat. All of these life lessons that we go thru on a daily basis. Learning how to handle stress and pressure, learning patience, and the bond with animals that no money can buy. She is learning how to deal with loss and grief. Sitting on the front porch watching the farmers come in and harvest what they've been growing all year long.

I thought about Scout at the National Junior High Rodeo Finals and how we were all so blessed to be there for that special event. I thought about the enormous amount of pressure put on a 13 year old who handled it like a professional the same way an Emergency Room nurse or doctor would handle a situation. Having the "balls and guts to enter" and the ridicule you sometimes get when it doesn't go as planned. It is pretty easy for someone sitting in the stands eating their "hot dog" to criticize. Of course they never had the guts or drive to take the chance?

Was it worth it? You bet it was.

Did you see that sunset? TJ and I watched a comet Friday night, just coming up from feeding and a comet "just passed our view." "Time Well Spent".

Us "Cowgirls", "rednecks", "Hicks", whatever you want to call us gals of passion for horses. We pay the farrier instead of pedicures. No facials, no manicures. Starbucks is a huge, huge treat. It is entree fees, diesel, the best feed, vaccines, and care for our ponies. (The classy ones at least) I realize these days there are all kinds of folks calling themselves "Cowgirls" but us real ones don't have to say anything, it's just who we are. Kind, compassionate, classy, and positive. We take care of the animals that take care of us.

So my answer is YES, "yeah" it was worth it all.... I wouldn't want it any other way. I would love Jason home full time of course but, other than that.

In closing I suppose I have to add "Butter my Butt, and Call Me a Biscuit," and please, pass the strawberry Jam!

My Intentions are always with Sincere Love,

Tracy D. :)

Is it worth it? This picture is the answer.

How many families have moments like this?

In this picture:

Roper: Scout at short round 5th in the Nation
AQHA Girl's Horse of the Year-
            Continental Sun Dust "Yellow"
2012 National Jr High Rodeo Finals (Gallop, NM)
Calf Pusher: Jason Hammond (her uncle)
In stands:
Jami (her mom)
Tracy (her aunt)
TJ (her cousin)

CHAPTER FOUR – MY FIRST BARREL RACE

By Tracy D. Hammond (the following are all actual events from the April 2004 famous "Walla Walla Barrel Daze")

Well, first let me tell you..... I'm no stranger to the rodeo scene

But what I was about to experience is where these girls spend a whole lotta green.

At 31, sis and I decided we'd enter our first big barrel race

We'd just ante-up to this fancy can chase!

If we wanted to get in the time onlies, we had to be there by eight

However, it was 08:30, we couldn't find the grounds, and shucks we was late!

A photo for finish, heck—we'd done this before,

But that was roping—not on two colts—better just stand back when you open the trailer door!

Do we pay first? Do we need a hat and long sleeved shirt? Heck, we just don't know?

Let's just saddle up, scrape off the mud and go with the flow.

Saddled just in time, and they are calling our name

It's not taking us long to realize; this is a whole different game.

Daytona ran great for his first time away from home

Beau wasn't so sure about the flags and banners in this tiny little dome.

Scout did fantastic, for this too was her first big barrel race

Course she's only five, and way more accustom to horses and dirt than ribbons and lace.

Along came Kelly and Cashie with a welcoming smile

When it comes to barrel races, this wasn't her first trip down the isle.

Finally the time onlies were done and we're heading for the stalls over by the track

Daytona was snorting at everything, despite being a grandson of Two Eyed Jack.

The horses are all settled and we're walking over to Kelly's fancy LQ

I called Jas and let him know this is NO place you'd find a good Buckaroo!

Time to relax, sit down and crack open a few

So what if it's only 10:30 am, we've got no curfew!

Five thirty pm, they'll start the show, the sweepstakes and Calcutta

Biankus and Judge Cash will take you to the pay window.

My money's on Dana, it was just last week I was so impressed with her practice run

These girls are coming in fast, who knew a 'barrel race' could be this much fun?!

Well, they are getting faster as each gal takes her turn

I've never seen so many outstanding jockeys, I'm just sitting there in awe…..taking in all I can learn.

They say we can get in the arena at 06:00 in the morn

I take a look around—I'm the only one with 'rubber' on my saddle horn!

I kind of chuckle to myself as I watch these 4 yr olds that look more like greyhounds trot around this petite cow shed

With all the fancy tack and gear, I wonder how many poor husbands are in the red?

I put my horse up and as I'm walking around I can't believe all the specialists I see

There are farriers, chiropractors, nutritionists and horses standing in magnetic therapy.

Oh boy, I tried to hold myself back but, you guessed it—I found myself a fancy LQ

But honey; it has a bed, a shower, an air conditioner….and even a heater for you?

What a great weekend we all had, we even came home with some extras…..a new trailer, some new splint boots for Scout, and I even bought a bling-bling coat detailed in hair-on hide

All I can wonder is, what else would we be doing if we didn't ride?

Driving home with a great big smile on my face

Beau and I won a check at My First Barrel Race!

CHAPTER FIVE – COWBOY "THE OLD MAN"

There's a beautiful vision that will never leave my brain. The kindness and love in those big brown eyes every night with that tiny hug and kiss added with that "special" can of grain.

His name is Cowboy but, she calls him the "Old Man". This almost 31 year old horse that has been in our family since the day his life began.

I wonder if dad knew the fate of this two year old colt the first time he saddled him in the round pen? They say sometimes you just know, but how could he ever predict how this history would go?

Cowboy and my sister, Jami, have been thru it all. Rodeos, buckles, a few large moves, a saddle, a broken arm and a week at WSU Vet hospital way too close of a call.

This little brown horse, a grandson of Two Eyed Jack at just about every roping or barrel race he was leading the pack.

And it wasn't just Jami that had all this education and fun. Along came her daughter, Scout, who learned first hand what it felt like to be number one.

Cowboy taught Scout how to ride, she won buckles, prizes, and an all around Saddle too.

If this little horse with the biggest heart could talk I sure what wonder what he would say all of the things he's seen, done, and traveled to in his day.

Between the hoop and hollar of the crowds at the rodeos, the laughs, giggles, and practical jokes, the "Eat my Dust" sign painted on his butt. The kind shoulder to cry on when the going got rough, to untying himself and getting out of a gate, that last you checked was shut?

"The Old Man", Cowboy, has done it all, parades, 4-H Horse Shows, rides out in the field, who knows how many people he's given their first ride on a horse.

Now TJ, my four year old daughter, is learning how to ride on him. I guess that is just part of his "planned" life course.

Well, Cowboy, "Old Man" I cannot thank you enough for all you have done, and the times you have been there for my family- I pray you have at least five more years in those big, brown, loving, eyes to complete history.

I Love you Cowboy!

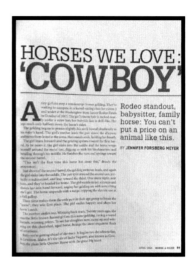

Mom contacted Horse & Rider about Cowboy and his accomplishments and they ran a long feature on him in their April of 2006 magazine.

CHAPTER SIX - KIONA'S DESTINY

I'll never forget the first day I saw that wild-eyed paint horse. He was in the round pen, hobbled, and saddled, but the way he was standing sure wouldn't put an experienced horseman at ease. His neck was arched and his head was high. His back had such a hump in it he looked more like a cat who'd just woken up and was stretching from a long overdue nap. Only Kiona, wasn't waking from a nap, he was untamed and his nostrils were flaring, his tail was slightly lifted with a crook right at the tip of the tail bone. He stood there paralyzed with his legs spread widely beneath him. It was cold and cloudy and the wind was blowing like crazy and with every twitch of his anxious ears one could tell that at any instant this magnificent keg of dynamite would explode.

Mom seemed to have no fear though; Dad grabbed an ear and she quietly put her left foot in that stirrup. Even though she was a veteran horsewoman and every instinct should of told her "what are you doing climbing on this stormy, spotted, son of gun?" Still she stepped on with poise. Mom's dream had always been to find a black and white paint horse and train it to run the barrels. It was the late 70's, early 80's and the paint horse was still a new and upcoming breed. Mom and Dad were searching high and low for a black and white patterned horse that was also bred to run. This seemed to be quite a mission, but Dad had been working out of town; in Pasco, Washington and he had run across this dark brown, and white paint, with the crazy eyes. His registered name was Kiona's Destiny. So… the legend began.

This story is so filled with love and passion one would be certain that I had to be making up this Disney-like tale. I can assure you that every detail is factual and all you'd have to do is whisper the name "Kiona" in this small Idaho town and most anyone affiliated with the equine species will know exactly who you were talking about.

Kiona's Destiny- Dad put at least 30 days on Kiona while he was over in Pasco, and when he felt he was ready to hand off to Mom they brought him home to Idaho. I remember the first-time Grandpa Henry saw Kiona and his wild eye; he assured Mom "that horse is going to hurt you."

Every time Mom kicked him into a lope he'd buck; however, she was determined to make that horse a champion and she rode him every day without fail. Soon Kiona learned that Mom was not a big, mean monster but that she was the one that fed him, nurtured him, and assured him that even through the spookiest of times and moments she'd take care of him. It did not matter if it was raining, snowing, or 20 below; Mom was going to ride that speckled pony and she did. She took her time training him on the barrels, and she took riding lessons from a local reiner and cow cutter; she was a good hand but there was always room for improvement, and Kiona had a destiny.

When Kiona was just five she entered that wild-eyed paint in the barrels at the Lewiston Roundup, a PRCA and WPRA approved rodeo at the time. It was his first big rodeo with a crowd, and hometown to boot. Kiona debuted running against another famous duo, Charmayne James and Scamper who won the rodeo, however Mom and Kiona had claimed a fifth- place check.

Time carried on; times were rough, and we had an old, beat-up Ford pickup and a two-horse trailer. There was a local barrel race every weekend. The entry fee was just three dollars for a time-only. Luckily in the local barrel club you could also receive points for the fast time. Mom would load up Kiona and Candy, my sister's Shetland pony, and to the barrel races we went. Riding Kiona was Mom's outlet; sometimes I stop and wonder how she could tolerate all that she did while we were growing up, but then I think of Kiona and I know how. That horse was her source of freedom and passion. And he sure kept her going for us kids.

You know they say all good horses have their weird, little quirks and Kiona had several. No matter how much he'd been hauled, rode, and taken places the outrageous eye was something he'd been born with and it made him who he was and he never lost it. Mom was the only one that could ride him for a very long time. He simply would not let anyone else on his back. You did not ride Kiona bareback… ever. Mom tried riding him bareback a couple of times and every time he'd arch his whole body, spread his legs, and crook that tail ready to blow at any moment. When my sister was still small but experienced Mom thought she'd toss her up on him one evening just to see what would happen. She was able to get her up there but, it took two hours to get my fearless, teary-eyed little sister off of him. He was a flighty creature. He must've been about fifteen or so when finally, I was in high school and enough like Mom that he'd let me start riding him, running the barrels and winning on him. By then we had a big, gooseneck trailer and were hauling five head of horses everywhere we went. Still, we always put Kiona in the last hole. Dad always said, "Always put Kiona in the back of the trailer so if you get in a wreck or a jam you can get him out first". Need-less to say Kiona didn't handle situations calm and quiet; it just wasn't his nature.

However, it was his nature to be loyal, and loyal he was to Mom and I. I can remember running him in the amateur section of the Lewiston Roundup and it being one of the greatest highs of my life. On a cool September, Saturday night I can remember running up the alley to the first barrel, whipping and spurring all the way knowing no matter how fast we went all I had to do was sit down and that "wild-eyed paint" would drop his hind quarters and wrap the first barrel. There was a standing ovation, the Snake River Thunder on the grandstands, and Kiona running hard all the way to the home gate.

There are so many little things that Kiona did that made him Kiona, like the way he'd arch his neck and look around with those crazy eyes just before he went in the arena, the way he pranced and stepped, and how athletic he was. He did so much for our family and my mother.

The spring of my senior high school year Kiona bowed a tendon on his front leg. I was unable to finish the high school rodeo season on him. I bought a new horse and Mom sold Kiona to my younger cousin. She used him for a few years and decided to sell him.

I was living in Nevada at the time and Mom was in California and remarried. I came up to Idaho and brought Kiona home. I called Mom and told her, her horse was going home with her again. After all, with her was his place. Mom kept him for a while and decided to sell him. She sold him to a lady that was going to do drill team and pack flags on him. I never did hear how that panned out, but Mom was still able to see him in a nearby pasture and stop to visit him from time to time.

Then it happened, that lady had sold him and no one seemed to know who had this paint steed or where he lived. Mom was remarried to no other than an equine veterinarian. It had been several years and Mom had been on several calls with him always kind of looking around corners hoping someday she'd see her wild-eyed friend. The years kept going by and we all figured it was a lost cause. Until, one day Dr. Haskin had an emergency call and asked Mom to go with him and assist. It was a local boarding facility and there around the corner she saw a brown and white paint. Could it be? She stopped, and looked again. It was him! It was Kiona! Of course she quickly found out who now owned her long lost friend. It was a young girl. Kiona was skinny and bony and he had several new, large, scars on his legs. It saddened her to see him like this, but she was happy to see him to say the least. She was able to call the girl that owned him and they soon met. Mom gave her a couple of lessons with Kiona.

Then one day Mom received a phone call, the young girl that owned Kiona had lost interest in riding and she could not afford to keep him anymore. She asked Mom if she'd like to just have him. Naturally, Kiona came back home to Mom's loving arms, (and grain).

I remember when I went to visit Mom one time. Kiona must've been twenty-two or so and of course I wanted to ride him. As I saddled him it seemed as though he had shrunk. He still had that high head set, arched neck, and elegant gliding way of walking. His mouth was a little harder than it had ever been but it felt good to be on him. Mom grabbed the video camera and asked me to take him for a spin around the barrels. It didn't take much coaxing and I took off towards the first barrel. Kiona bucked, he must've been happy to be there too. Mom and I both had a good laugh and put him away.

Mom decided Kiona should be turned out somewhere so once again she sent him back to Idaho to stay at one of my sister's friends and retire out on her acres of pasture. The friend kept Kiona for a couple of years. Then one day she called my sister and told her Kiona was dropping weight. She was feeding him Equine Senior and had his teeth done but the weight wasn't staying on. He had cancer on his penis and it was determined that, that might be a large cause of the weight loss. I was back in Idaho and my husband and I had plenty of room at our house for Kiona. I thought, well, I can put weight on anything and I did try, but Kiona had no teeth left and it was clear it was time to say good-bye to our loyal, old friend. I had to think about it for a couple of weeks and talk to Mom, but we all knew it was the right thing to do. Kiona's Destiny is buried on my place, but his legend will always live on.

CHAPTER SEVEN – JUST LET HER RIDE

Just Let Her Ride!

Some call it an obsession, maybe it really is an addiction, but if you come between a cowgirl and her horse you're gonna have some contradiction.

The bond between a woman and her steed I can't begin to explain, but try and stop her from rid'n and you'll have better luck stop'n a freight train.

"So why not let her ride."

Waylon said it best when he said "Men that don't know him won't like him and men that do won't know how to take him."

I can't point out just one thing; about these four legged creatures that'll draw a girl in. Don't know if it's the freedom, the speed, their smell, or their kind, gentle, eyes or maybe the rush of adrenaline.

"Just let her ride."

For years now men have been trying to figure out why they get fed after that bushy tailed friend and why when she's not riding him, she's talking about him, and why everything revolves around that dang ole horse. Don't fight it .....

"Just let her ride."

If you're not a cowgirl you just may never understand. Remember, that's why you loved her in the first place, she's strong, independent, and so passionate about what she does.

So when she says "I'm gonna go ride," don't cuss.

"Just let her ride."

Most cowgirls have a heart of gold and aren't afraid to step up to the plate when the truth needs to be told.

So don't take her all wrong cause she's loved you; all along.

"Just let her ride."

Sorry boys if you are looking for answers, or reasons why, or even a cure; I'm pretty sure you're plumb out of luck. One thing you can count on, she'll always have a love for that species they call the equine. So "just let her ride" and you'll get along mighty fine.

Tracy Hammond 08/06

CHAPTER EIGHT – COUNTRY LIVIN'

Just for fun… "Country Livin'"

Well the garden's been hoed and the lawn's been mowed.

The flowers, the little maple tree, the zucchini, and the animals all have feed and water.

Just about time to go in and cook up some French toast; for my daughter.

Soon as I'm done filling up the pigs' mud holes,

I'll have the dough arisin' for Rynearson Rolls.

Grab my beloved Crockpot and toss in a Reeves Ranch Roast,

Now all this that I'm sharing is not to brag… or boast….

I'm just blessed to see another sunrise out in the country today.

Sharing my gratitude and dropping down to my knees to pray.

"God, thank you for Jason, our home, animals, and of course TJ."

Tidy up the kitchen real quick and run a load of wash, but I'm really looking forward to saddling up soon.

Check the calendar date, dang it's July already? What happened to June?

Scout and I run the calves in and load em' in the chute, I'm thinkin' they have cheat in their eyes, perhaps it is just a lot of flies?

I text Pam a picture and Scout checks the internet. Now I'm pretty certain our first case of bovine pink eye… we've just met.

So LA 200, some powder ,and black patches with glue,

Jared shows up to help throw em and tie em too.

Swim lessons, groceries, and errands to run,

I should have TJ practice her math and writing but, us girls we would rather load those calves back up, rope, and have fun.

Night time now and dinner chores are complete, a glass of red wine, and get ready for bed.

All of the day's blessin's of friends, family, and animals are running through my head.

Looking forward to another day of Country Livin' answered prayers and blessin's given.

Amen~ ☺ Love, Tracy D.

CHAPTER NINE – AND GOD MADE A HORSE

August 30 · 2016

I haven't written for a while and today I was inspired by this little buckskin I've been riding. I thought to myself "this horse needs someone he can trust" and…then I thought well, who better than his thirteen- year- old owner, Emmy. Then I got to thinking about all the life lessons this little grandson of Hollywood Dunit could teach this young lady and of all the stresses and pressures a 13 year old girl has in this day and age, and what a blessing it was that she could turn to this horse for her education. Without further a-do. Here's what I came up with. Inspired by "Whiskey and Emmy", and all of us other horse crazy girls from ages 5 thru 84 and still saddling up! (Carolyn Cook)

So God Made a Horse...

God knew she was going to need someone to share her dreams, her fears, her tears, her failures and victories with, so God made a horse.

God knew she had to learn how to be strong, and kind, and courageous, all at the same time, So God made a horse.

God knew she needed to learn how to be responsible and put others needs ahead of her own, So he created a horse.

God knew she was going to have tough days at work and school beyond her control and when she arrived home she was going to need a big, brown, kind, eye to comfort her, So... He created a Horse.

God knew she was going to have a life altering event and she was going to need that "normal", that routine, of throwing hay twice a day and filling troughs, and saddling up to get away from it all. So God created a horse.

God knew she was going to marry a man strong enough to hold onto the reins and yet soft enough to know she'd stop in her tracks with one tender touch. So God created a Horse.

God knew it wasn't going to be easy, so she would need to learn how to be firm, gentle, and yet disciplined too. So he created the Horse.

God knew she needed to meet the right people with the same passion and gratitude for his magnificent creation. So God created a Horse.

God knew she needed self-confidence and that sometimes she would have to take chances to get the job done. So God made a Horse.

God knew that someday she would have to know exactly how to get up, dust herself off, and get back on again. So God created a Horse.

God knew he was going to need someone he could trust, someone to Love him and care for him, protect him, and be his partner through all of the ups and downs.

So God Created The Cowgirl...

Amen,
Love, Tracy D.

CHAPTER TEN - IN THIS ARENA DIRT

In this arena dirt... we get to put the rest of the world on PAUSE for a while.

In this arena dirt... you'll find parents who know where their teens are at night because they are right there with them, running the chute, loading cattle, and holding goats.

In this arena dirt... the aroma of good ole fashioned Hammond Ranch dinner lingers from the kitchen.

In this arena dirt... you'll discover my sweet husband running the chute and my niece, Scout, perfecting her timing. TJ will be lining calves and absorbing it all. You'll capture me with a rope in my hand (or loading calves, or running the chute, and/or coaching, more than likely hooping and hollern' about yet another "sweet run" made). My sis, Jami, on another colt, fine tuning the next potential legend.

In this arena dirt... parents get to turn off the pressures of the work place, smell cow manure, laugh, and unwind with good friends. (Sometimes even get kicked by a calf just to keep it real)

In this arena dirt... we say please and thank you, we teach soft hands and jerking on horses' mouths is not acceptable. We put words like "TRY, GRIT, and INITIATIVE " into action and make it a HABIT.

In this arena dirt...Hot and stressed out horses get to stop, let out that big sigh, and lick their lips. They remember they like and enjoy their jobs.

In this arena dirt...So many "Firsts" first time on a horse, first catches, "first time he's been roped off of" "first time I've roped in twenty years!" "First time a bunch of city kids smelled the unforgettable scent of burning hide and branding calves, or witnessed "cutting nuts" to make a bull calf a steer.

In this arena dirt... one Sunday afternoon, my friends surprised me with dinner and buckets to pick rock. Jason and I have hauled sand, shoveled sand, spread sand, and groomed sand.

In this arena dirt...I've prayed a lot, I've sweat a lot, been poured on, and been soaked and cold, all with TJ riding right beside me. I've cried tears of joy watching her ride and Emmy sync with Whiskey what a sight! Oh yeah...I've even bucked off here once too!

In this arena dirt...real friendships have been made and strengthened. Good working dogs are manifested and appreciated.

In this arena dirt...confidence is built, character is revealed, and Champions are grown.

In this arena dirt...Love lives and thrives, true friends sweat with ya and help you achieve your goals.

In this arena dirt...prayers have been answered and I'm so excited for the next chapter of this BLESSED ARENA DIRT...

> Amen-
> Love,
>   Tracy D.
>   (Written December 10, 2016)

CHAPTER ELEVEN- IT WAS QUITE A SPOT TO BE IN BUT…

It was quite a spot to be in but, it was going to happen she honestly believed it would.

It was not going to be easy but, with Faith she knew she could.

So she kept praying, visualizing, and sharing as her conscience said she should.

Steadfast with a genuine and compassionate heart often times her motives were quite misunderstood.

Tears were shed along the way yet she stayed persistent in prayer, for she knew there was a reason that man had been nailed to the wood.

She kept doing her best to do the right thing, for this time the outcome had to be even more than just good.

So what is the conclusion? And you want to know just how does it end?

Well, stick around for more and we'll soon celebrate my sweet friend.

Love,

Tracy D.

3-19-98

Dear God, Jesus, and Angels,

These are my desires - I want our own beautiful Ranch w/ beautiful horses and good looking cattle. I want our house to be new/or remodeled, clean, bright and cheery. I want to have two wonderful children that grow up happy and positive and hardworking. I want Jason and I to be able to stay at home and work, to have our bills paid on time w/no worry of how we would pay them. I want to get up in the Am & go feed in the quiet clean air. I want to be a prosperous, well respected horse woman. To Rodeo in the summers and do what we love to do. I want to wake up in the am, feed, go for a walk, ride and clean my sunny, bright house with lots of flowers and I want to spread that good feeling to my friends & family. God what I really desire is that place I drew. I don't know how long it'll take you but, six months time to get it started would be great. The shorter Jas & I have to go through figuring out how to pay bills & doing jobs we don't like the better. I know we would have such a beautiful place and we'd both be almost like in heaven. God, Jesus and your angels please give this a try, we won't dissapoint you.

ABOUT THE AUTHOR

A cowgirl since day one, Tracy was born and raised in Lewiston, Idaho and sitting in the saddle before she could even crawl. Blessed with parents who were dedicated to raising and training fine horses and living the western lifestyle, this outdoor loving gal was destined for greatness in the arena. When the acclaimed horse "Cowboy", came to retire on the Hammond ranch, he afforded her a lifetime of love and sport that has forever changed her and many other girls that have followed. After her younger years at horse shows and learning the fundamentals of horsemanship, Tracy moved up to high school and college rodeo and even fulfilled some dreams by hitting the amateur scene for a few years.

Thanks to the keeper of the stars she met and married her best friend and Nevada buckaroo, Jason Hammond. They now make their home in Lewiston with their beautiful daughter TJ where they spend the majority of their time outside in arena dirt and country air with their five horses, three dogs, three goats, six laying hens, and a various number of roping calves and barn cats.

Tracy realized her dream of making her passion her paycheck in 2015 when she started her own business training others how to rope and ride. "Cowboy", at the experienced age of 35, is still the trusted steed that she starts all of her beginners on, as she knows he will always take care of his rider.

Grateful for a life that offers Tracy the chance to do what she loves with her daughter right by her side, she is gratified when she witnesses a child's realization of their hard work and the fruits of their labor. Her "time well spent" shows when victory is achieved and the pride of accomplishment shows on their faces.

As decades pass and new seasons begin, Tracy still spends every day roping in the summer sun. She mostly enjoys the little family rodeos they attend with TJ and several of Tracy's students and good friends. It's a lifestyle she does not take for granted and she can't imagine waking up every day without the chance to throw hay to her crew, with her loyal black and white sidekick Zip trotting alongside. In the stillness of her home as she is spending time in prayer and writing each morning, she feels that grace has truly won. Watching the sunrise as the soft nickers of her horses break the silence, she is reminded of God's provision for her family and the majestic environment they are blessed to call home.

Made in the USA
Las Vegas, NV
08 January 2021